I0012149

Android XR

Google's New AI Glasses – Everything You Need to Know

A Guide to the Next Frontier of Technology and the Artificial Intelligence Revolution in Your Everyday Life

J. Andy Peters

Copyright ©**J. Andy Peters, 2024.**

All rights reserved. No part of this publication may be reproduced, distributed, or transmitted in any form or by any means, including photocopying, recording, or other electronic or mechanical methods, without the prior written permission of the publisher, except in the case of brief quotations embodied in critical reviews and certain other noncommercial uses permitted by copyright law.

Table of Contents

Introduction

The world of technology has been evolving at an astounding pace, with new innovations continuously reshaping the way we live, work, and interact with the world around us. But there's one leap on the horizon that promises to change everything—an era where our physical reality merges seamlessly with the digital world. This is the promise of XR—Extended Reality. At the heart of this revolution is Android XR, an ambitious project by Google, built on a foundation of cutting-edge artificial intelligence and augmented reality. It's not just another new tech fad. Android XR represents the next step in how we'll engage with the world, offering a richer, more immersive experience that goes beyond traditional devices.

The introduction of Google's AI glasses, designed to work in harmony with Android XR, takes us one step closer to the world of sci-fi films. Imagine wearing a pair of glasses that, instead of just helping you see better, superimpose digital information right before your eyes. They provide real-time insights into your surroundings, translate languages as you speak, and even offer suggestions for better ways to live your life, all without the need for a screen. This fusion of AI, augmented reality, and wearable technology isn't just a glimpse into the future—it's happening now.

But what does this mean for us, the users? Why should we care? Because this isn't a technology that's meant to replace the way we interact with the world. Instead, it's a tool designed to enhance every moment. Whether you're navigating a new city, cooking dinner, or simply organizing your daily tasks, Android XR promises to be the digital assistant that's always there, in the most intuitive, seamless way possible. The way we interact with technology is about to undergo a transformation—one that blends the digital and physical worlds in ways we could never imagine before.

Throughout this book, we'll take you on a journey through the XR revolution. We'll explore the technology behind Android XR and Google's AI glasses, break down the impact of augmented reality and artificial intelligence, and show you how this fusion will make a difference in your everyday life. You'll learn how these innovations will enhance productivity, enrich entertainment experiences, and provide solutions for everyday challenges in ways that were once the stuff of science fiction. The XR era is not a distant future; it's something we're stepping into today.

As we venture further into the pages, you'll come to understand why Android XR and Google's AI glasses are more than just the next trend—they are the future of technology. And this future will change everything.

Chapter 1: Entering the XR World – A New Reality

When we talk about **XR**—Extended Reality—we're stepping into a world where the lines between what's real and what's digital blur. XR is an umbrella term that encompasses a variety of immersive technologies that expand our perception of reality, taking us beyond the traditional screen or device. But what exactly is XR, and how does it relate to other technologies like Augmented Reality (AR), Virtual Reality (VR), and Mixed Reality (MR)? Let's break it down.

Virtual Reality (VR) is the most immersive of these technologies. When you put on a VR headset, the digital world completely surrounds you, blocking out your physical environment. It's like stepping into an entirely different world—a virtual one where you can explore, interact, and even live out experiences that would be impossible in real life. Whether it's gaming, training simulations, or virtual tours, VR takes you away from reality and places you into a fully simulated environment.

On the other hand, **Augmented Reality (AR)** is a technology that layers digital information over the real world, enhancing your perception of it. Instead of fully immersing you in a virtual space, AR adds digital objects or information to your physical surroundings. Think of the popular AR apps that allow you to view directions on your phone screen, or the Snapchat filters that overlay digital images on your face. AR helps you see the world differently but doesn't isolate you from it.

Mixed Reality (MR) sits somewhere between AR and VR. With MR, digital objects not only appear in your real-world environment but can also interact with it. It's not just about seeing digital elements in your space; it's about these elements being integrated into the world as if they truly belong there. For instance, imagine using a digital object that you can move, touch, and manipulate, and it responds to your environment in real-time—like having a virtual ball bounce off a real wall.

Extended Reality (XR) is the umbrella term that brings together AR, VR, and MR under one roof. It refers to all the technologies that either extend or enhance reality in some way, whether that's by immersing you in a completely virtual world, augmenting your current surroundings with additional information, or merging the two in ways that feel almost magical. XR is the gateway to blending the digital with the physical in a seamless, natural way.

What makes XR so special is its ability to transcend the boundaries of traditional screens. Instead of relying on a monitor or a smartphone, XR uses your surroundings as part of the experience. It's a more **immersive**, **interactive**, and **intuitive** way of engaging with digital content. Imagine walking through a city and having the buildings, streets, and even people around you interact with digital overlays, guiding you through your day without ever needing to look at a device. The world becomes your interface.

This seamless blending of the real and the digital is what makes XR so exciting. It's not about isolating you from the physical world like VR does; it's about augmenting and enhancing your reality to create richer, more meaningful experiences. XR doesn't just add digital content; it makes that content feel like it's always been a part of your world.

The world of wearable technology has come a long way since its early days. What started as rudimentary devices designed to track steps or measure heart rate has evolved into a powerful, transformative tool that blends seamlessly into our daily lives. The story of wearable technology isn't just about gadgets—it's a journey toward creating devices that augment human potential and provide experiences we once only dreamed about.

Take a step back in time to **Google Glass**—one of the first bold ventures into the world of wearable computing. When Google Glass launched in 2013, it promised to bring the power of the internet to your eyes, providing notifications, GPS directions, and even hands-free calling, all displayed on a tiny screen in the corner of your vision. While the device was revolutionary in its potential, it faced numerous challenges, including privacy concerns, limited battery life, and an awkward form factor that left many skeptical of its practicality. Despite its short-lived commercial journey, **Google Glass** set the stage for the wearable tech we're witnessing today, planting the seed for a new kind of interaction with the digital world.

Fast forward to the present, and Google is again at the forefront of this revolution, but this time with a much more refined approach. Enter **Android XR**, a platform that has evolved from the lessons learned with Google Glass and the advancements made in augmented reality (AR) and artificial intelligence (AI). Android XR isn't just a new device; it's the next step in an ongoing journey to enhance our relationship with technology and our environment. This platform represents a significant leap forward, merging the power of AI, augmented reality, and wearable hardware into a single, cohesive experience.

Samsung and **Qualcomm** have played pivotal roles in bringing Android XR to life. Both companies have been at the forefront of wearable technology, pushing the boundaries of hardware design and processing power. Samsung, with its history of innovation in the tech world, has contributed significantly to the development of sleek, ergonomic XR headsets and glasses, ensuring that they are not only functional but also comfortable and stylish. Qualcomm, on the other hand, has provided the cutting-edge chips and processing power that make these devices run smoothly, ensuring the performance is seamless, responsive, and powerful enough to handle the demands of AR, AI, and immersive experiences.

Together, Google, Samsung, and Qualcomm are creating a future where wearable tech becomes an integral part of our daily routines. But why is **XR** the natural next step for computing?

The evolution of computing has always been driven by the need to make our interactions with technology more intuitive and natural. In the early days, we interacted with machines using punch cards and terminals. As computing progressed, we moved to personal computers, laptops, and tablets—devices that provided more power and functionality but were still confined to screens. Smartphones were the next big leap, combining a computer, a camera, and an internet connection in a single portable device. But even with these advancements, the interaction still requires us to look down at a screen and navigate with our fingers.

XR is the next logical step in this progression because it takes the screen out of the equation altogether. Instead of interacting with technology through a device, XR integrates technology directly into our surroundings, making it more natural and intuitive. Imagine walking down the street and receiving a text message not on a phone screen, but projected directly into your field of view. Or envision looking up directions in an unfamiliar city, and having them overlaid onto the buildings around you, guiding you step-by-step without ever needing to pull out your phone.

XR doesn't just improve how we use technology—it changes the very way we experience the world. It turns the entire environment into an interactive interface, where information, entertainment, communication, and even work tasks are no longer confined to a device in your hand. With wearable technology like Android XR, the future of computing is one where technology is an extension of ourselves, seamlessly integrating with the real world in ways that were once only possible in science fiction.

As we move beyond the smartphone era, **XR** represents a new frontier—one that will reshape everything from how we work and communicate, to how we learn, play, and experience the world around us. The dream of truly immersive computing, where the digital and physical worlds coexist and interact fluidly, is no longer a far-off vision. It's here, and it's already beginning to change the way we live.

Chapter 2: Google's Vision for AI-Powered Glasses

The development of **Android XR** wasn't born in isolation; it was a collaborative effort by some of the biggest players in the tech industry. The platform's evolution was shaped through deep partnerships, most notably with **Samsung** and **Qualcomm**, two companies whose innovations in hardware and processing power have consistently set new standards in the tech world. These partnerships weren't just about combining forces—they were about forging a new direction for the future of wearable tech, where augmented reality (AR) and AI would seamlessly blend into our everyday lives.

Samsung, a leader in consumer electronics and mobile devices, has long been at the forefront of hardware development. For years, they've pioneered designs that are both cutting-edge and user-friendly. With their expertise in producing sleek, high-performance devices, Samsung was an obvious choice for Google to partner with in building the physical hardware for Android XR. Through this collaboration, the platform has evolved into a product that is not only powerful but also ergonomic and practical, making the concept of wearable augmented reality much more feasible and appealing to the average consumer. The **Android XR** headsets and glasses, created with Samsung's input, are designed to look like everyday wearables, not clunky pieces of tech, which is a crucial factor in their adoption by the public.

At the same time, **Qualcomm**, known for its prowess in mobile processors, became an indispensable part of this journey. Qualcomm's **Snapdragon XR** chips have been specifically designed to power augmented reality experiences. With the capability to process large amounts of data and provide high-speed connectivity, these chips are the engine that makes Android XR's immersive experiences possible. Without such robust processing power, the sophisticated technologies that fuel Android XR—like real-time data processing and AI-driven insights—wouldn't be feasible. Qualcomm's contributions ensure that Android XR remains not only a visionary concept but a functional reality.

Yet, it's not just the hardware that sets **Android XR** apart. The platform's true power lies in the **Gemini AI**, which acts as the brain behind the entire system. Gemini is the key to unlocking the full potential of Android XR, blending AI with augmented reality to create experiences that feel as intuitive and natural as everyday interactions. Through Gemini, Android XR doesn't simply present information—it **understands** the context of the user's environment and adapts in real-time. Whether it's offering directions, translating languages, or even suggesting the most efficient way to complete a task, Gemini makes the technology responsive to the needs and desires of the user.

For instance, imagine you're in a foreign country, trying to decide what to order from a menu. With

Android XR, Gemini can read the menu in real-time and provide contextual information, such as which dish is spicier or which option suits your dietary preferences—all without needing to reach for your phone. It's not just about receiving information; it's about having the digital world assist you, seamlessly, in the physical world.

What makes this even more powerful is that Gemini doesn't just react to your inputs—it **anticipates** your needs. If you're setting up a new shelf in your home, Android XR can guide you step-by-step, offering advice on where to place the shelf and even suggesting the best tools for the job, all based on what it sees around you. In this way, **Gemini** enables Android XR to be a personal assistant, always on hand, always ready to make your life easier. Whether it's through real-time problem-solving or offering intelligent suggestions, Gemini AI makes Android XR not just a device, but a living, breathing companion that enriches every interaction.

With these combined forces—Samsung's hardware expertise, Qualcomm's processing power, and Gemini AI's intelligence—**Android XR** is poised to be a game-changer. It represents the culmination of years of advancements in technology, all coming together in a single device that promises to redefine how we interact with both the digital and physical worlds. Unlike previous forms of augmented reality, which were often cumbersome and disjointed, Android XR offers an experience that's fluid, intuitive, and, most importantly, useful.

As Google moves forward with this ambitious project, the possibilities are endless. **Android XR** is not just about creating another gadget; it's about fundamentally changing the way we live, work, and play. By offering seamless integration with everyday tasks, powerful AI-backed interactions, and immersive augmented reality experiences, Android XR has the potential to revolutionize the tech landscape. For Google, Samsung, and Qualcomm, this is just the beginning—an entry point into a future where augmented reality is a natural part of the fabric of daily life.

When we think about wearable technology, particularly glasses, we often imagine bulky gadgets that stick out, feeling more like a novelty than a practical device. Yet, **Google's AI Glasses**, powered by **Android XR**, challenge that assumption entirely. These glasses aren't just designed to be futuristic—they're crafted with a real sense of practicality in mind. They're sleek, portable, and, most importantly, made to be worn throughout the day without feeling like an encumbrance. In fact, the goal for these glasses was never to be something you "wear" just for specific occasions, like a virtual reality headset. No, Google has built these glasses with all-day use in mind, making them the ultimate wearable device.

Unlike traditional headsets or augmented reality gear, which are often too cumbersome to be worn for long periods, the **Android XR glasses** are incredibly lightweight. Designed with everyday wear in mind, they feel like a regular pair of glasses but with a powerful set of features hidden in their frames. The frames themselves are sleek, with the kind of style and comfort you'd expect from high-end eyewear, making them something you can wear from morning to night, whether you're in a business meeting, out for a walk, or watching your favorite show. The portability of these glasses is key—since they're designed to function as all-day wearables, it's important that they're light enough to forget you're even wearing them. The technology that powers them is seamlessly integrated into the design, so you don't feel like you're carrying a mini-computer on your face.

At the heart of this cutting-edge wearable technology is **real-time data processing**. This isn't just about displaying information in front of your eyes; it's about interacting with your world in a way that feels natural, intuitive, and incredibly efficient. The **Android XR glasses** don't just show you static information—they process the world around you in real-time. With the power of **Gemini AI**, these glasses are capable of understanding your environment and adapting accordingly. Whether you're walking down the street, navigating through a crowded shopping mall, or sitting at a café, the glasses can interpret your surroundings and offer valuable insights, all without interrupting your daily life.

The real magic comes when you start using the glasses. Imagine walking through an unfamiliar city, and as you glance around, you see directions pop up, guiding you to your destination, without needing to pull out a phone or navigate through menus. Or imagine you're in a meeting, and the glasses subtly display key information about the topic being discussed or the people in the room. With **real-time processing**, the **Android XR glasses** can detect the context in which you're operating and deliver the most relevant information at the exact right moment.

But what truly sets these glasses apart is how **Android XR** acts as a platform not only for users but for developers as well. While Google has designed these glasses to be as user-friendly and intuitive as possible, they've also created a flexible ecosystem for developers to build upon. By offering a rich set of tools and resources, **Android XR** allows developers to create new, immersive experiences that can make daily life even more interactive and productive. Whether it's apps that help with productivity, fitness, entertainment, or even specialized tools for professionals, the possibilities are endless. The platform is designed to be open, allowing for constant innovation and evolution, which means that the glasses can grow and adapt over time, adding even more value to your daily routine.

Unlike other forms of AR or VR, where the experience is often isolated from the real world, **Android XR glasses** blend the digital and physical in a way that feels seamless and natural.

You're not just interacting with virtual worlds—you're enhancing your real-world experiences, making the mundane extraordinary. Whether it's getting real-time translations, having instant access to information, or simply having a digital assistant that understands what you need before you even ask, these glasses are built to make your life easier, more informed, and ultimately, more connected.

What makes Google's AI glasses different isn't just the technology inside them, but how seamlessly they integrate into your daily life. They're not just futuristic gadgets—they're designed to be an indispensable part of your world. With real-time processing, a sleek and portable design, and a platform that encourages endless innovation, **Android XR glasses** are set to redefine what it means to be "connected." And as the tech continues to evolve, the possibilities for these glasses are boundless.

Chapter 3: How Android XR Will Change the Way You Live

Imagine stepping into your day with a pair of glasses that not only let you see the world around you but also enhance how you interact with it. **Android XR** is transforming everyday tasks by introducing **real-time AI assistance** into the most natural parts of our lives. Whether it's something as simple as reading a group chat or as complex as navigating a new city, these glasses provide you with hands-free solutions that feel like an extension of your own thoughts.

Picture this: You're walking through the park, and your phone buzzes with an update from a group chat. Normally, you'd have to stop, pull out your phone, and read the message. But with **Android XR glasses**, you don't need to interrupt your stride. Instead, a soft prompt appears right in front of your eyes, summarizing the key points of the message. No need to glance down at a screen or disrupt your flow—your **AI-powered glasses** are already working in the background, making sure you stay connected without lifting a finger.

This real-time assistance extends far beyond text messages. You can ask your glasses about anything from restaurant reviews to reminders about appointments, and the AI will respond seamlessly, almost like having a personal assistant right in your line of sight. Whether you're in a meeting, out for a walk, or at the grocery store, your glasses are always ready to lend a hand, giving you the information you need exactly when you need it.

One of the most exciting features of **Android XR** is its ability to deliver hands-free interaction with **AI-driven functionalities**. Imagine traveling abroad and not knowing the local language. Normally, you'd have to pull out your phone and fumble with translation apps. But with **Android XR glasses**, the AI can automatically translate signs, menus, or even conversations in real-time. You simply look around and receive instant translations, displayed right in your field of view.

No need to search for an app or worry about slow connections; the information you need appears almost effortlessly.

Navigation is another area where the glasses truly shine. With **Android XR**, you no longer need to stare down at a map or a phone screen while walking or driving. As you move, real-time directions appear in your glasses, guiding you without interrupting your environment. If you're on foot in an unfamiliar city, a small, dynamic arrow can float ahead of you, showing you the way to your destination. You can simply follow the visual cues, and the AI will keep updating the directions as you move. Whether you're walking through a dense crowd or exploring a new neighborhood, navigation becomes intuitive and seamless, making you feel like you're always in the right place at the right time.

But the real power of **Android XR** comes when you think about how it can help with **smart decision-making**. As you go about your day, the

AI adapts to your environment and offers recommendations that improve your decisions and actions. Whether you're unsure about what to wear, looking for a specific item in a store, or deciding on the best route to take, **Android XR** offers guidance based on context and real-time data.

For example, while shopping, if you pick up an item, the AI can show you reviews, prices at other stores, or even let you know if there's a better option nearby. If you're wondering whether to grab a quick coffee or head straight to your meeting, the AI can factor in your schedule, traffic conditions, and nearby locations, offering a recommendation that helps you maximize your time. The decision-making process is enhanced by the wealth of information available to you through the glasses, allowing you to make better choices faster and more confidently.

In a sense, **Android XR** empowers you to be more present and efficient. You're not distracted by technology; instead, it flows into your life in ways that feel natural, supportive, and unobtrusive. Whether it's answering a quick question or offering deeper insights into your environment, the AI works with you, not against you, ensuring that your day runs smoothly.

With **Android XR**, the act of navigating your surroundings becomes as intuitive as breathing. Gone are the days of juggling a map or struggling with your phone while walking through an unfamiliar neighborhood. With **XR glasses**, everything you need to know about your location and surroundings is right in front of your eyes, seamlessly integrated into your field of vision.

As you step out onto the streets of a new city or even your own neighborhood, the glasses provide **real-time maps** and **location-based advice** directly in your view. Instead of awkwardly holding up a phone to follow a map or looking at a screen while trying to make sense of your next move, you simply look ahead, and the **XR glasses** offer dynamic, contextual directions. Whether you're navigating a busy city street, finding a hidden café, or tracking a walking trail through the woods, your glasses provide clear, constantly updated guidance. A small arrow or visual cue floats in your line of sight, showing you exactly where to go, and adjusting based on your position, ensuring that you never feel lost.

But the power of **Android XR** isn't just in getting you from point A to point B. The glasses act as your personal assistant, offering advice and insights as you go about your day. When you're heading to a meeting or an event, the **AI** can give you up-to-the-minute updates, such as suggesting the fastest route or even recommending places to stop along the way. If you're traveling to a new location, the glasses might highlight nearby points of interest, from restaurants to historical landmarks, ensuring that you don't miss out on key experiences. It's like having a guidebook and a navigation tool all rolled into one, offering useful suggestions at the perfect moment.

One of the most exciting integrations within the **Android XR** glasses is the **Google Lens**, which allows you to interact with the world around you in completely new ways. You can simply look at an object, a building, or even a piece of text, and the glasses will instantly provide relevant information. If you're walking down the street and spot a piece of art or architecture, **Google Lens** can identify it for you, giving you details about its history, artist, or significance. This feature truly brings the world to life, allowing you to explore and learn more about your surroundings with a simple glance.

The **Live View** feature also enhances the navigation experience, giving you an augmented reality (AR) overlay of your route directly in your line of sight. As you walk, the glasses can superimpose directional arrows and helpful annotations on the real-world environment, turning ordinary streets and landmarks into a vibrant, interactive experience. Whether you're trying to find your way through a crowded airport or exploring an unknown neighborhood, **Live View** turns every journey into an immersive experience.

Another standout feature of the **Android XR glasses** is **real-time translation**, powered by **Google Translate**. Imagine you're traveling in a foreign country and you come across a sign in a language you don't understand. With **Android XR**, you simply look at the sign, and the glasses instantly translate the text into your preferred language, displaying it in your line of sight. It's as if the world itself is speaking your language. From menus in restaurants to street signs and even conversations with locals, the integration of **Google Translate** removes language barriers and makes you feel more connected to the places you visit.

Together, these features make **Android XR glasses** not just a tool for navigation, but a gateway to an enriched, more informed experience of the world. Whether it's finding your way around, discovering hidden gems, or breaking down language barriers, the **XR glasses** empower you to explore with confidence, all while keeping your hands free and your eyes focused on the world around you.

Chapter 4: The Future of AI in Augmented Reality

The true magic behind **Android XR** lies in the seamless fusion of **AI** and augmented reality, with **Gemini AI** at the core of this innovation. This advanced technology doesn't just enhance the reality around you—it interprets and interacts with it in real-time, transforming your surroundings into a rich, dynamic experience that feels personal and tailored to your needs.

Gemini AI, developed by Google, is the driving force behind the **XR glasses'** ability to perceive and understand the world around you. This isn't a static form of artificial intelligence; instead, **Gemini** processes the signals from your environment and makes sense of them in ways that are intuitive and responsive. When you wear the glasses, **Gemini AI** is constantly at work, analyzing the visual cues, objects, and movements in your field of view. It's as if you have a personal assistant who not only understands your voice commands but also actively reads the room, adjusting its suggestions based on your actions and context.

Imagine walking into a new café for the first time. With **Gemini AI** running in the background, it can recognize the ambiance of the place, offer suggestions from the menu, or even translate the text on the walls into your language. The glasses are constantly processing visual data, interpreting it, and offering assistance in real time. Whether it's a product label, a landmark, or a building, the AI knows how to present the right information at the right moment. The AI doesn't just passively observe; it actively enhances your experience by turning the ordinary into the extraordinary, making everything around you smarter, more interactive, and more informative.

But **Gemini AI**'s role isn't confined to giving directions or providing information. It opens up new dimensions of **interactivity** within the **XR** platform. Through the glasses, digital content doesn't just sit on a screen; it exists alongside the physical world. You can interact with virtual objects, overlay digital tools onto real-world scenarios, and even manipulate environments as if they were tangible. Imagine trying to assemble furniture—**Gemini AI** can guide you step-by-step, offering holographic visuals that show you exactly where to place each part, as if it were physically in your hands. This immersive engagement creates a synergy between the digital and physical, allowing you to interact with technology as naturally as you would with the real world.

Perhaps one of the most captivating aspects of **Android XR** is its ability to create **spatialized memory**—the idea of reliving past experiences in a completely immersive way. Through **Gemini AI**, users can revisit memories and experiences by spatializing them in augmented reality. For instance, imagine seeing an old video or photo and not just viewing it on a screen but experiencing it in 3D, as if you were back in that moment. You could walk around the space, interact with the environment, and even look at the scene from different angles. This ability to spatially relive memories will not only enhance personal storytelling but will also redefine how we interact with our past. It's an experience that bridges the gap between memory and reality, turning snapshots of the past into fully realized, interactive moments.

As **Gemini AI** continues to evolve, the potential for creating an increasingly **immersive** and **informative environment** grows. Imagine being in an unfamiliar city, and the glasses not only provide directions but also offer detailed historical context as you pass landmarks. Or think about the possibility of working in a new field and having the AI provide real-time technical assistance, explaining things as you go, offering tips, and making recommendations based on what it observes in your surroundings. The **AI** acts as a guide, a teacher, and an assistant all at once, bringing new depth to your daily life.

In essence, the role of **AI** in **augmented reality** isn't just about adding extra layers of digital information on top of the real world; it's about making your environment smarter, more responsive, and more interactive. With **Gemini AI** powering **Android XR,** the world around you becomes a dynamic, evolving space that adapts to your needs, helping you navigate it in ways that were once the realm of science fiction.

The arrival of **Android XR** and its **AI glasses** has the potential to reshape the way we experience the world, shifting the boundaries between **the physical** and **the digital**. As technology rapidly evolves, it's not just about making tasks more efficient or enhancing entertainment—it's about transforming **how we connect**, **learn**, and **engage** with the world around us. The social and cultural implications of XR technology are profound, and its impact on human interaction could be nothing short of revolutionary.

One of the most immediate effects of **XR** on our daily lives is the way it changes **how we consume information**. In an age where we're constantly inundated with data, the ability to have instant access to relevant information in the form of augmented reality could fundamentally alter our interaction with the world. The **Android XR glasses** are designed to filter out the noise, offering real-time, context-sensitive information that's tailored to the situation at hand. Instead of having to pull out your phone or sit in front of a computer to search for something, you'll have critical information delivered directly in your line of sight. Whether it's an update on a group chat while you're working or information about a street you're walking down, this new form of information consumption blends seamlessly with daily life. It's intuitive, unobtrusive, and designed to enhance, rather than disrupt, the flow of everyday activities.

Along with changing how we gather and process information, **Android XR** will also impact **how**

we communicate. The power of **AI** combined with **augmented reality** has the potential to dissolve the barriers that typically exist in virtual interactions, making them feel more authentic and immersive. Imagine attending a virtual meeting where instead of looking at a screen, the people you're interacting with appear directly in your environment as though they were standing beside you. Or, when speaking with friends, instead of merely sending texts or pictures, you could use XR to send visual messages or holographic representations of yourself, making communication feel more engaging and human. This will be particularly valuable for long-distance relationships or remote teams, creating a sense of closeness that traditional forms of communication, like video calls, have struggled to achieve.

Perhaps one of the most compelling aspects of **Android XR's AI glasses** is the way they **bridge the gap between reality** and **virtual experiences**. By integrating the real world with digital content in a way that feels natural, XR glasses allow users to interact with virtual elements as if they were part of their physical surroundings. The line between the two worlds becomes increasingly blurred, creating a new, hybrid reality. This fusion of the real and the virtual will lead to new ways of thinking about existence and interaction. Virtual experiences will no longer feel like a separate, isolated realm—they will be an extension of your everyday life, enhancing the present moment without detracting from it.

This technology's influence won't be limited to entertainment or personal use. The future of **remote collaboration**, **education**, and **entertainment** stands to be revolutionized by **Android XR**. For example, in the **workplace**, remote collaboration could become far more immersive and effective. Instead of just looking at a screen during a conference call, XR glasses will allow people to meet in a **virtual office** space, interact with 3D models, or engage in collaborative design work as if they were in the same room. The ability to **see** your colleagues in 3D, **move** around virtual objects, or even gesture toward shared documents will make remote work feel far more natural and effective than current communication tools allow.

In the field of **education**, XR has the potential to radically change how we teach and learn. Imagine a classroom where students can experience lessons through fully immersive, interactive environments. History lessons could take students to ancient civilizations, allowing them to walk through historic cities. Science students could explore molecular structures or visit the planets in 3D. The sense of presence provided by XR will make education more engaging and memorable, allowing for a deeper understanding of complex topics through first-hand experience. Additionally, these immersive learning experiences will be available to anyone with an internet connection, potentially reducing the barriers to access that have traditionally existed in education.

Entertainment, too, will undergo a profound transformation. While virtual reality has already begun to make waves in gaming and immersive experiences, **Android XR** takes this a step further by blending virtual content with the physical world. Imagine being able to walk into a movie scene, where the characters and environment react to your movements. Instead of merely watching a film, you could **be part of it**, experiencing the action as though you were inside the story. The same applies to gaming, where the distinction between the physical and virtual world vanishes, allowing you to physically move through and interact with your game environment. Whether it's through sports, music, art, or other forms of entertainment, XR will bring a new layer of interactivity that fundamentally changes how we experience leisure and creativity.

The **social and cultural impact** of XR is undeniable. As **Android XR** becomes more accessible and widely adopted, it will reshape the ways we live, work, learn, and play. These changes will not only affect the **individual user** but will also challenge **societal norms** and **cultural practices**, potentially reshaping everything from work dynamics to social relationships. The **future** of communication, education, and entertainment is no longer confined to the realm of speculation—it's here, it's happening, and it's transforming how we experience the world.

Chapter 5: The Potential Applications of Android XR

As the digital world becomes more integrated into our physical spaces, **smart living** is emerging as a new way to interact with our homes and environments. Thanks to the combination of **AI**, **augmented reality**, and **wearable technology** like **Android XR**, everyday tasks are being redefined, making our lives not only more convenient but also more efficient and enjoyable.

One of the most promising aspects of this new era is **home automation**. Gone are the days when managing household tasks meant flipping switches, manually adjusting thermostats, or constantly checking on appliances. With **Android XR** and its **AI-powered** capabilities, your home becomes a smarter, more responsive space that caters to your needs. Imagine being able to control lighting, adjust the temperature, or even start your washing machine simply by asking your **XR glasses** or making a gesture. These intelligent systems integrate seamlessly with your home's infrastructure, learning your preferences and adjusting accordingly to make your living space more comfortable without needing constant input.

But **smart living** isn't just about comfort—it's also about **health monitoring**. With **Android XR** on your face, you gain access to real-time health insights that help you stay on top of your well-being. Imagine an intuitive system that reminds you to take your medication, tracks your physical activity, or even monitors your heart rate or blood pressure while you go about your day. This is not only a tool for keeping tabs on your health but also a personal health assistant that continuously helps you make smarter lifestyle choices. Whether you're managing chronic conditions or simply trying to live a healthier life, the seamless integration of **AI** and **XR** into your environment provides you with personalized feedback in a way that feels natural, empowering, and proactive.

Then there's the growing role of **AI-powered assistance** in **work productivity**. No longer do you need to juggle multiple devices to stay organized. With **Android XR**, you can merge work and life tasks into a unified experience. Whether you're working from home, managing a project, or brainstorming new ideas, your **AI glasses** can offer real-time updates on meetings, tasks, or deadlines, all while offering suggestions, scheduling appointments, and even organizing emails without lifting a finger. The **XR glasses** allow you to visualize complex data, create virtual whiteboards for brainstorming, or even share your screen with colleagues, all within your field of vision. This makes collaborating with remote teams feel as easy and intuitive as working in the same room.

Home improvement and **DIY** tasks are also receiving a major upgrade with **XR** technology. One of the most exciting possibilities is the **AI-powered assistance** available for home repairs, renovation projects, and even cooking.

Imagine attempting a complex repair task, like fixing a leaky faucet or installing new shelving. Instead of struggling to follow written instructions or watching a YouTube tutorial, you can get **real-time, step-by-step visual guidance** directly in your line of sight. As you look around your home, the XR glasses will overlay instructions, point to where tools are needed, and provide feedback as you complete each step. This transforms DIY projects from intimidating to manageable, giving anyone the ability to tackle home improvement tasks with confidence.

When it comes to **cooking**, the possibilities are equally impressive. **Android XR** can assist in everything from meal planning to the actual cooking process. Imagine starting with a recipe where the **XR glasses** provide you with a 3D model of each ingredient, tell you how much of each item to use, and even walk you through the preparation steps. As you cook, the **AI assistant** can adjust the temperature of your oven or stove, ensuring your dish is prepared exactly as the recipe suggests. These systems also help you navigate the kitchen hands-free, meaning you don't need to touch your phone or look down at a tablet while handling raw ingredients.

With **smart living**, **Android XR** isn't just about making life easier—it's about making it smarter. The way we interact with our environments will no longer be limited to traditional interfaces or simple touch screens. Thanks to **XR**, our environments will become **intelligent**, **interactive**, and deeply personalized. Whether you're automating your home, monitoring your health, working more efficiently, or tackling DIY projects, **Android XR** brings **AI-powered convenience** directly into your daily routine, allowing you to get more done with less effort, and creating a seamless connection between you and your surroundings.

As we look ahead, the potential of **smart living** with **XR** is only just beginning to unfold. This technology will not only transform how we live but also the quality of life we experience. The ability to blend the digital and physical worlds will change how we see our homes, our workspaces, and our health. The future is here—and it's all about making our lives **smarter, simpler, and more connected** than ever before.

In the ever-evolving world of **technology**, **Android XR** opens up a new dimension for entertainment and exploration. Gone are the days when your **television** or **video games** were confined to flat screens. With **XR glasses** and **AI** powering these experiences, the line between the real world and digital content begins to blur, creating a truly immersive world that you can engage with like never before.

Imagine watching your favorite **TV shows** or **movies** in a completely new way. Instead of being limited to the small screen, **Android XR** transforms your living room into a **cinematic experience**. The glasses overlay digital elements onto your surroundings, making you feel as though you're sitting inside the scene itself. This level of immersion goes far beyond the traditional 2D viewing experience. Whether you're watching an action-packed movie, a gripping documentary, or a sci-fi thriller, you're no longer just watching the screen—you're part of the experience. The blend of **augmented reality** with traditional media offers a level of engagement that's not possible with older technologies, making you feel as if you're actually in the world of the story.

When it comes to **gaming**, **XR** truly shines. Instead of being tied to a console or a stationary device, **Android XR** glasses allow you to dive into **augmented and virtual reality games** that respond to your real-world environment. Games become immersive experiences where digital worlds exist alongside physical space. Imagine playing a **puzzle game** that overlays clues around your house, or a **strategy game** where you can physically walk around the map, making decisions in real time. With **XR**, the gaming world isn't confined to a screen anymore; it's all around you, transforming your environment into a fully interactive playground.

Beyond entertainment, **Android XR** revolutionizes the way we explore the world. **Google Maps** has long been a tool for finding directions and navigating unfamiliar places, but with **XR** integration, it's now a **3D experience**. Instead of looking at flat 2D maps or GPS directions, you can see your surroundings overlaid with real-time navigation cues. **Android XR** uses augmented reality to project walking or driving directions directly onto the road, guiding you step by step, just as if you had a personal assistant at your side. The **AI-powered system** constantly adapts, offering new routes based on your location, the time of day, and traffic conditions. This level of dynamic assistance makes getting from point A to point B smoother, safer, and more intuitive.

The enhancement doesn't stop with navigation. **Google Photos** now comes to life in 3D, allowing you to view and experience memories from a completely new perspective. Instead of flipping through static images on a screen, **Android XR** enables you to immerse yourself in your favorite photos, turning still images into interactive 3D scenes. Whether it's revisiting a **family vacation** or seeing your old photos of a past event, these memories are transformed into **dynamic, spatially aware experiences** that bring your past to life like never before. Each photo can become an environment you can explore, walk through, and even interact with, offering a deeply nostalgic yet futuristic experience.

In addition to daily exploration, **Android XR** introduces the future of **virtual tourism**. With just a pair of glasses, you can visit landmarks across the world without leaving the comfort of your home. From the **Great Wall of China** to the **Pyramids of Giza**, these landmarks are no longer distant concepts; they're places you can experience first-hand through your **XR glasses**. Whether it's walking through the **Colosseum** in Rome or taking a guided tour of the **Eiffel Tower, XR-powered virtual tourism** allows you to explore these magnificent sites as if you were there. The **immersive 3D rendering** combined with real-time data makes it feel like you're truly standing in the middle of these historical sites, opening the door to limitless exploration. You can even visit museums, art galleries, and natural wonders, experiencing them in a **highly interactive, educational** way that traditional media simply cannot match.

Whether you're exploring new worlds through entertainment, navigating your local environment with enhanced maps, revisiting cherished memories, or virtually touring global landmarks, **Android XR** redefines the way we experience both digital and physical spaces. It's a fusion of technology, **artificial intelligence**, and **augmented reality** that makes your entertainment and travel experiences richer, more exciting, and, most importantly, **immersive**. The world as you know it is being transformed, and with **XR glasses**, every journey—whether real or virtual—becomes an adventure of its own.

Education has always been a transformative power, shaping minds and preparing individuals for the future. Now, with the advent of **XR glasses** and the integration of **AI** technology, the way we learn, teach, and experience education is undergoing a radical transformation. No longer confined to textbooks and traditional classrooms, **Android XR** opens up new possibilities for **interactive, immersive learning** that transcends geographical and physical barriers.

In classrooms across the world, **XR glasses** are enabling a whole new form of **hands-on learning**. Imagine a science student learning about the human circulatory system not by reading a chapter, but by exploring a 3D model of the heart and blood vessels right in front of them. They can see blood flow in real-time, watch how oxygenated blood travels through the body, and even perform virtual dissections—all through their **XR glasses**. This level of immersion brings abstract concepts to life, offering students a deeper understanding of complex subjects by allowing them to engage directly with the material.

The power of **XR** extends far beyond the classroom. With **AI** assistance integrated into the **XR glasses**, students can now have real-time help as they work through problems. Need assistance with a math equation? The **AI** will not only guide you through the solution step by step but will adapt its teaching method to your individual learning style. Struggling with a concept in history? The AI can provide contextual information, related historical events, and visual aids to enhance comprehension. This level of interaction makes learning personalized, effective, and tailored to each student's pace.

One of the most exciting developments in education is the ability to bridge the gap between in-person and **remote learning**. **XR technology** enables students and teachers to connect in virtual classrooms, even if they are thousands of miles apart. Imagine attending a virtual class where the teacher is not just speaking through a screen but is actually **present in the classroom with you**—their avatar interacting with you and your peers. Whether it's a small seminar or a large lecture, **XR** allows for **immersive** interaction, making remote learning more engaging and less isolating. Students can ask questions, participate in group discussions, and even collaborate on projects in a way that feels **natural** and **real**, breaking down the barriers of distance.

XR is also empowering **students** to break free from the confines of traditional education settings. Field trips are no longer limited to physical locations; with **XR glasses**, students can virtually visit historical landmarks, explore underwater ecosystems, or journey to the farthest reaches of space—right from their classrooms. Imagine a history class where instead of reading about

Ancient Egypt, students walk through the streets of **Luxor**, interact with holographic representations of **pharaohs**, and witness key events unfold. This immersive experience creates lasting memories and deeper connections to the material, making learning feel far less like a chore and much more like an adventure.

Moreover, for students with disabilities or special needs, **XR technology** can offer customized educational tools that cater to their specific requirements. **Visual learners** can benefit from 3D models and interactive simulations, while **auditory learners** can engage with real-time spoken assistance and guided exercises. The ability to design personalized learning experiences means that no student will be left behind. The **AI** built into the **XR glasses** can assess a student's progress, suggest adjustments to the lesson, and ensure that the content is accessible and engaging for all.

As traditional educational structures face challenges, whether it's overcrowded classrooms, high dropout rates, or insufficient resources, **XR technology** offers a solution that empowers both students and teachers to take education into their own hands. With real-time, **immersive** experiences and interactive AI assistance, **Android XR** makes learning more dynamic, personalized, and accessible than ever before. The potential for **remote collaboration**, hands-on activities, and enriched digital content brings education to a whole new level—one that breaks down barriers, fosters collaboration, and makes learning an exciting, interactive journey.

In this rapidly changing world, **Android XR** will continue to redefine what's possible in education, empowering a new generation of learners and educators to break free from the limitations of traditional classrooms. Whether it's a child learning to read or an adult seeking new knowledge, **XR** is not just the future of education—it's the present, unfolding in real time.

Chapter 6: How Android XR Could Shape the Future

As we look to the next decade, it's clear that **Android XR** and its integration of **AI glasses** are not merely passing trends—they are poised to revolutionize every facet of our lives. The way we interact with the world, work, and communicate will undergo a profound transformation. From **healthcare** to **transportation**, **education** to **entertainment**, **XR glasses** will make their mark, not just as a tech novelty, but as essential tools woven into the fabric of daily existence. The future is **extended reality**, and **Android XR** is at the forefront of this seismic shift.

At the core of this evolution is the **AI glasses** themselves. What was once a vision for the future is quickly becoming a reality. **Android XR** glasses could become as ubiquitous as smartphones, integrated into our daily routines seamlessly. Picture this: waking up to real-time updates on your **health stats**, receiving navigation directions while cooking breakfast, attending virtual meetings while on a walk, and seeing live translations of foreign-language signs while traveling abroad—all through a device so discreet it's almost invisible. The **AI** embedded in these glasses will continuously learn your preferences and adapt to your habits, offering personalized recommendations and assistance wherever you go. The world will no longer be something you simply observe but something you actively engage with through the lens of **extended reality**.

But the impact of **XR glasses** will stretch far beyond the consumer experience. **Industries** across the globe will see their workflows and processes reshaped by this technology. In **healthcare**, doctors and medical professionals will use **AI glasses** to view patients' medical histories, access real-time diagnostic data, and even receive hands-free guidance during surgery. Surgeons could use augmented reality to overlay 3D images of organs or veins directly onto a patient's body, increasing precision and reducing the chances of error. With AI and XR combined, medical professionals will have a level of insight and interaction that will make patient care safer and more efficient than ever.

In the **transportation sector**, **XR glasses** will change the way we drive, navigate, and travel. Imagine a world where your glasses provide **augmented reality navigation** while driving, offering real-time traffic updates, hazard warnings, and even the ability to analyze road conditions ahead of time. This could reduce accidents, ease congestion, and make transportation safer and more efficient. **AI-driven transportation** could also transform **public transit systems**, allowing for real-time scheduling updates and interactive travel plans based on current conditions. The potential for **XR glasses** to revolutionize logistics and delivery services is enormous as well, providing workers with hands-free, intuitive navigation as they manage routes and deliveries.

In **education**, **XR** will reshape traditional learning environments. Virtual classrooms, real-time feedback, and hands-on experiences will become the norm. No longer limited by geography, students will have access to **immersive learning environments**—from virtual field trips to interactive history lessons—making education more engaging and accessible to learners of all backgrounds. Teachers, too, will benefit from **AI-assisted teaching** platforms, enabling them to reach more students with personalized instruction and real-time support. The distance between traditional classroom setups and modern, interactive environments will blur completely, creating a learning experience that is both intuitive and immersive.

The **entertainment industry** is also on the cusp of a revolution thanks to **Android XR** and **AI glasses**. From gaming to movies, XR glasses will offer **immersive experiences** that go far beyond anything we've seen before. **AI-powered**

interaction will allow players to engage in **interactive storytelling**, making games more dynamic and personalized. Moviegoers could watch films in **3D** environments, stepping into the scenes and interacting with the content. **Concerts**, sports events, and other live performances will also be transformed with **augmented reality**, offering a level of **immersion** previously reserved for science fiction.

For all of these industries, the integration of **AI** will continue to be the driving force behind the **XR revolution**. As the glasses evolve, so too will the AI systems that power them. With each interaction, these systems will become more **intuitive**, **context-aware**, and **personalized**—adapting to the user's needs, environment, and desires. This will transform **XR glasses** from a tool into a **companion** that actively improves the quality of life for every user.

Looking to the **next decade**, we can only imagine the possibilities that **Android XR** and its ecosystem will unlock. **Artificial intelligence**, **augmented reality**, and **wearable tech** will work in tandem, creating experiences that were once limited to imagination. The future will be more **immersive**, **connected**, and **adaptive** than we ever thought possible. As **XR glasses** become commonplace, we will have the tools we need to make smarter decisions, improve our health, expand our learning, and enhance our entertainment. It won't just change how we interact with the world—it will change the world itself.

The **XR revolution** is just beginning, and **Android XR** will lead the charge, making what was once thought impossible a part of our daily lives. It's an exciting time to look ahead, as the **next decade** promises to be one of unprecedented innovation and transformation.

As we embark on the promising journey into the **XR era**, we must also confront the **challenges** and **ethical dilemmas** that accompany the rapid advancements of technology. While the potential of

Android XR and **AI glasses** is extraordinary, several obstacles need to be overcome to ensure that these technologies reach their full potential and serve society responsibly. These challenges range from concerns about **privacy** and **data security** to more practical hurdles like **user comfort**, **battery life**, and the **technological infrastructure** required to make **XR** a seamless part of everyday life.

One of the most pressing challenges revolves around **privacy**. As XR technology becomes more integrated into our daily lives, it will continuously collect vast amounts of data, from personal interactions and preferences to physical movements and environmental details. This raises significant concerns about who owns this data, how it is used, and how to ensure that it's protected from unauthorized access. **Google**, as a leader in AI and wearable technologies, will need to adopt robust data protection policies and work closely with regulators to safeguard user information.

Furthermore, consumers will demand transparency about how their data is handled, making it imperative for companies to establish clear privacy guidelines and protocols. **AI-driven decisions** within the XR environment could also face scrutiny: how do we ensure that these systems remain fair, unbiased, and free from manipulation? The ethical implications of real-time data collection and AI decision-making will require ongoing discussion and development of global standards to protect users while maximizing technological benefits.

In addition to privacy concerns, **data security** will be a critical factor in the success of **Android XR**. The interconnected nature of **XR glasses** and their reliance on cloud computing for real-time processing means that sensitive data is constantly being transmitted and stored across various platforms. Protecting this data from cyber threats will be paramount. Encryption protocols, secure cloud infrastructures, and advanced AI security measures must be designed to guard against hacking, identity theft, and other cybercrimes. While **AI glasses** can offer a world of convenience, they also open new vectors for attacks that need to be addressed as part of the development process.

On the more **practical** side of things, several **technological barriers** still need to be overcome before **XR glasses** can become the mainstream, everyday device that we envision. The current size of **XR glasses**, while much smaller than previous models, is still bulky when compared to traditional eyewear. **Google** and its partners will need to refine the design further, creating glasses that are not only powerful but also sleek and comfortable for all-day wear. The integration of **advanced sensors** and **displays** within such a small frame presents its own challenges, particularly in maintaining a high level of performance while keeping the product lightweight and stylish. **Battery life** is another hurdle—XR glasses require a lot of power to run **real-time data processing** and **immersive augmented reality** applications.

The current battery technology will need to evolve to ensure that users can wear their glasses for extended periods without worrying about frequent recharging.

User **comfort** will also play a significant role in determining the success of **Android XR**. **AI glasses** must not only fit comfortably on a variety of face shapes but also ensure that the weight, balance, and design do not cause discomfort or strain. With extended use, wearers may experience headaches or eye fatigue, so ensuring a natural and **ergonomic fit** is critical. If these barriers are not addressed, adoption rates for **XR glasses** could be significantly hindered.

Another challenge lies in the **XR ecosystem** itself. The platform for **Android XR** must evolve to include contributions from a variety of **developers**, **partners**, and **third-party applications** in order to create a comprehensive ecosystem. **App developers** will need to create experiences that integrate well with the XR environment, offering new capabilities in gaming, education, health, communication, and more. Furthermore, as the platform matures, **third-party hardware** manufacturers will likely step in to create accessories and complementary devices that expand the functionality of the glasses, such as improved audio systems, specialized sensors, or additional augmented reality content. The **collaboration** between **Google**, **Samsung**, **Qualcomm**, and other partners will be crucial in shaping the development of the XR ecosystem, ensuring compatibility across devices and creating an ecosystem where users have access to a wide range of tools and applications.

Despite these challenges, the opportunities are boundless. **Android XR** has the potential to revolutionize how we live, work, and play. It's not just about wearing a device on your face; it's about enhancing your connection to the world around you. Imagine a future where AI and XR combine seamlessly to make your life easier, more productive, and more enjoyable. Developers will have the opportunity to create applications that can radically change industries, from **medicine** to **education**, **business**, and **entertainment**. **XR** could redefine how we experience everything from **learning environments** to **virtual travel**, and developers have the power to create new kinds of digital content that will immerse users in ways never before possible.

Additionally, as the ecosystem grows, the possibility of more **cross-platform integration** emerges. With collaboration, we could see **Android XR** interacting with other major systems and devices, like smart homes, automobiles, and even medical technology, further improving the synergy between the physical and digital worlds. **AI-powered tools** could offer unprecedented levels of assistance in daily life—anticipating needs, providing real-time feedback, and making decisions that enhance productivity and efficiency across industries.

As the **XR revolution** progresses, the combined efforts of tech companies, developers, and regulators will be essential in overcoming these challenges and creating a world where these technologies can thrive responsibly. In the coming years, the successful integration of **AI glasses** into the mainstream will require navigating complex issues around privacy, security, design, and ecosystem collaboration. However, if these obstacles can be tackled, the rewards will be extraordinary: a future where the boundaries between the physical and digital worlds blur, enabling users to experience life in ways previously thought impossible.

Chapter 7: Getting Started with Android XR

As the excitement around **Android XR** grows, many are wondering when they will finally be able to get their hands on these groundbreaking **AI-powered glasses**. While there's no official release date set yet, tech enthusiasts and early adopters are eagerly awaiting the day when **Android XR glasses** will transition from prototype to product. Fortunately, details about the **launch plans** and **anticipated releases** are slowly starting to surface, providing some insights into when these cutting-edge devices will become available for consumers.

One of the most anticipated releases in the **Android XR** journey is the **first device** to hit the market: **Samsung's Project Muhan**. This project, developed in collaboration with **Google** and **Qualcomm**, is expected to be the **pioneer** of **Android XR glasses** and set the standard for the future of wearable AI technology. Though specifics about the timeline remain unclear, industry insiders expect **Project Muhan** to launch sometime in **2025**, with some reports suggesting that early versions might be unveiled in limited quantities earlier, possibly by the end of **2024**. Samsung's role in the development of the **XR glasses** has been pivotal, especially when it comes to the **hardware** side of the equation. Samsung is known for its innovation in display technology, and this partnership promises to deliver **advanced optics** and **cutting-edge processing power** within the glasses themselves.

The **key features** of **Samsung's Project Muhan** are likely to be a game-changer in the world of augmented reality. The **glasses** will likely be equipped with **AI-driven capabilities** that can process information in real-time, overlaying digital content onto the physical world with stunning clarity. With **Google's Gemini AI** working behind the scenes, these glasses will offer **personalized assistance**, real-time navigation, and seamless interaction with digital content—all while maintaining the sleek and portable design that users have come to expect from **wearable tech**. The combination of **high-quality displays**, **advanced sensors**, and **long-lasting battery life** will be essential for creating an experience that feels natural and intuitive, without the discomfort or distraction of clunky tech.

For those who can't wait to try out the new **Android XR glasses**, **beta testing opportunities** will be available, though in a limited capacity. Early adopters will likely have the chance to get involved through **invitation-only programs** or **pre-order campaigns** as part of Google and Samsung's efforts to gather feedback and refine the product before a full launch. **Beta testers** will likely experience a version of the glasses that is not yet perfect but offers a chance to get a sneak peek at the future of **augmented reality**. The goal for these testers is to provide valuable insights into areas such as **user experience, comfort, battery performance,** and **AI functionality**—all of which will play a critical role in ensuring that the final product meets user expectations.

As for the **launch plans**, the glasses will likely be introduced at major tech events like the **Google I/O conference** or **Samsung's Galaxy Unpacked event**, where key details about the product and its features will be officially unveiled. Once available for general release, the **Android XR glasses** will likely be sold through **Google's official channels**, including the **Google Store** and possibly through major retailers or wireless carriers who will offer the glasses as part of a larger tech bundle.

As demand for the glasses grows, the product will likely expand to various regions, with **global availability** expected in the months following the initial release. **Pricing** will play a significant role in determining the product's success. Based on the advanced technology and features included, it's anticipated that the glasses will be positioned as a

premium device, likely in the range of **$500 to $1,000**. While this price range may be steep for some, the **Android XR glasses** will likely offer a range of functionalities that justify the cost, especially when it comes to AI-driven productivity, immersive entertainment, and real-time assistance.

Despite the high price tag, the excitement surrounding the **Android XR glasses** continues to build, with consumers eager to be among the first to embrace this new frontier of **wearable tech**. As with any cutting-edge technology, the rollout of **Android XR** will be gradual, with some early adopters getting access to the glasses sooner than others. However, once the glasses are officially released, they are expected to rapidly gain traction in the market and become the next big thing in tech.

Using Android XR in your daily life is about unlocking a new way to interact with the world around you, blending the digital and physical in a way that enhances both productivity and enjoyment. These AI-powered glasses are designed to seamlessly integrate into your routine, helping you get the most out of your day.

First, setting up your XR glasses is a straightforward process, designed to be user-friendly so that even those who aren't particularly tech-savvy can get started quickly. Pairing the glasses with your smartphone or tablet is a breeze, typically done via Bluetooth or a dedicated app that acts as a bridge between the devices. From there, you'll be guided through a series of prompts to ensure the glasses are adjusted to your preferences. Whether it's screen brightness, font size, or audio settings, everything can be customized to suit your comfort level. For users who already own other smart devices, the integration is even more seamless. Whether you're connecting to your smart home, syncing with fitness trackers, or linking up to other gadgets, Android XR allows you to keep everything connected in a simple and intuitive way.

Once your environment is set up, using the AI glasses to assist in your daily tasks becomes a powerful tool. Picture this: you're cooking, and your hands are busy with ingredients. Instead of fumbling with your phone or asking someone for help, the glasses provide real-time guidance through recipes, step-by-step. If you're on the go, they can guide you to your next appointment, offering turn-by-turn navigation right before your eyes, without having to stop and look at your phone. At work, AI can assist you by summarizing emails, sending reminders, and even helping you manage your calendar.

The real beauty of Android XR lies in its ability to give you the information you need, when you need it, without interrupting your natural flow. As you move through your day, the glasses continuously learn your habits, adjusting their suggestions and insights accordingly. For example, the AI might notice that you frequently check for traffic updates during your morning commute and will start presenting those updates automatically before you even ask. This type of real-time, contextual assistance makes the glasses more than just a wearable—they become an extension of your mind, helping you make decisions faster and more efficiently.

By optimizing your daily tasks through AI-driven suggestions, Android XR not only makes your life easier but smarter. It's not just about having technology in your hands—it's about having it right in front of your eyes, transforming the way you interact with the world and helping you make better decisions, faster. Whether you're handling work emails, managing your schedule, or navigating through a crowded city, Android XR ensures that technology is a seamless, intelligent partner in your daily routine.

Conclusion

As we stand on the cusp of a new era in technology, Android XR offers a glimpse into a future that once seemed like science fiction. The fusion of artificial intelligence, augmented reality, and wearable technology is not just a fleeting trend but the foundation of the next great leap in how we interact with the world around us. This revolutionary technology is not confined to the realm of tech enthusiasts and early adopters; it has the potential to reshape the daily lives of billions.

Looking ahead, Android XR will continue to evolve and expand, paving the way for an era where AI glasses are as ubiquitous as smartphones once were. The road ahead promises exciting advancements as Google, alongside its partners like Samsung and Qualcomm, refines the technology, pushing the boundaries of what's possible. In time, this technology will integrate seamlessly into every aspect of our lives—from enhancing productivity and communication to transforming how we learn, entertain, and navigate the world.

For now, Android XR stands as a cutting-edge tool for those fortunate enough to be at the forefront of this revolution. Early adopters are already experiencing the power of AI-assisted, hands-free interaction, but the full potential of this technology is still unfolding. As XR glasses become more refined and accessible, they will transition from niche devices to everyday essentials, creating a more connected, efficient, and immersive world. Imagine a future where every moment is enhanced by the intelligence of AI, where the world around you constantly adapts to your needs, where your devices intuitively understand and assist you in ways you never thought possible. That future is closer than you think.

Android XR will not just change the way we use technology—it will change the way we live. By seamlessly integrating augmented reality into our everyday environment, these glasses will allow us to experience the world in entirely new ways, making us more connected, informed, and efficient. Whether you're navigating a new city, staying productive at work, or simply enjoying a movie, Android XR promises to enhance your experiences, offering a deeper connection to both the digital and physical worlds.

Now is the time to start exploring this exciting new frontier. The XR revolution is coming, and it's ready to transform how we experience the world. For those who want to stay ahead of the curve, now is the moment to get involved. Dive into the world of Android XR, embrace the potential of AI-powered glasses, and be part of a future that promises to be more connected, more immersive, and more efficient than ever before.

The future is here, and it's waiting for you to experience it. Don't miss out on this technological leap—embrace it, explore it, and get ready for a smarter, more immersive tomorrow.

www.ingramcontent.com/pod-product-compliance
Lightning Source LLC
LaVergne TN
LVHW051538050326
832903LV00033B/4316